# THE SOULFUL BALANCE

## EMBRACING SPIRITUALITY IN A MODERN WORLD

### AASHIMA GOD'S CHILD

To the Divine Source,
whose boundless love, grace, and silent wisdom have
illuminated every step of my journey.
You are the eternal flame within me—the still voice in
chaos, the calm in the storm, and the strength behind my
every word.
In moments of solitude, in whispers between heartbeats,
You have spoken to my soul.
This book is not just mine; it is a humble offering of the
truth You have revealed through sacred stillness, quiet
reflection, and divine awakenings.
Every word written is wrapped in the gratitude of
knowing You, and every page turned is a prayer for others
to find You too.

To my beloved family and cherished loved ones,
your unwavering belief in me has been both my anchor
and my wings.
You've held my dreams as gently and fiercely as your love
for me—steadfast, patient, and strong.
Thank you for being the foundation upon which this
dream could rise.
In my moments of doubt, your presence was my reminder
of love's power to heal, to fuel, to transform.
Without you, these pages would be silent; with you, they
sing.

And to you, dear reader—
the radiant soul seeking clarity in confusion, purpose in
the mundane, and peace amidst the noise of modern
life—this book is for you.

May it feel like a warm embrace, a trusted guide, and a
gentle reminder that you are never alone.
The light you seek is already within you. It always has
been.
In your stillness, you will remember. In your journey, you
will rediscover.
Let this book meet you like a sacred friend—walking
beside you, witnessing your unfolding.

Let it be more than just a book.
Let it be a mirror of your soul—a sanctuary of truth, a
beacon of hope, and a companion of the heart.
May its words stir something timeless within you, and
may its essence stay long after the final page is turned.

With all my love,
Aashima, God's Child

# Contents

# Foreword

In a world driven by deadlines, digital distractions, and the relentless pursuit of success, the gentle voice of the soul often fades into the background. We rush through our days trying to keep up—yet deep inside, something yearns for stillness, depth, and meaning.

"The Soulful Balance" is a powerful invitation to slow down, breathe, and reconnect with the part of yourself that never stops whispering: there's more to life than this.

With poetic sincerity and grounded wisdom, Aashima, God's Child, bridges the gap between the spiritual and the practical. Drawing from real-life stories, heartfelt reflections, and transformative practices, she gently guides you toward a life where purpose meets presence, and ambition aligns with inner peace.

Whether you're a busy professional, a seeker in transition, or simply someone longing to live more mindfully, this book meets you where you are—and walks beside you as a trusted companion on your journey inward.

You'll find yourself pausing, reflecting, and reconnecting—with yourself, with the present moment, and with something greater than you've ever imagined.

Let this book be your mirror, your light, and your reminder:

You don't have to choose between the spiritual and the modern world. You can walk with grace in both.

This isn't just a book. It's a homecoming.

— Aashima, God's Child

# Preface

The idea for this book was born from my own sacred struggle—the silent tug-of-war between spiritual yearning and modern responsibility. I have always felt a deep connection to something greater, a presence that whispered to me in quiet moments. Yet like many, I found myself caught in the whirlwind of deadlines, expectations, and the endless noise of daily life.

There were times I felt fragmented—spiritually awake, yet disconnected from my own soul. That ache became my turning point.

I came to realize something profound: spirituality isn't a destination outside of our lives—it's the path that runs through it. It doesn't ask us to escape the modern world. It asks us to be fully present in it, while staying connected to our inner light.

This book is a mirror of my own journey to find that soulful balance—a harmony between doing and being, between ambition and stillness, between the outer world and the truth that lives within.

Whether you're beginning your spiritual path or have walked it for years, I offer you this book as a companion. May it speak to the part of you that longs for peace in chaos, purpose in routine, and presence in the present.

You don't have to choose between being spiritual and being modern.
You are allowed to be both—and thrive.

With all my love and light,
Aashima, God's Child

# Acknowledgements

Writing The Soulful Balance has been more than a creative endeavor—it has been a transformative, soul-stirring journey. And like every meaningful path, I did not walk it alone.

First and foremost, my deepest gratitude flows to the Divine Source—God, whose infinite love, wisdom, and grace have illuminated every page of this book. You are the still voice that whispered when I doubted, the light that guided me when I felt lost, and the strength behind every word I've written.To my beloved family—thank you for being my unwavering foundation. Your love, patience, and quiet faith have lifted me higher than I ever imagined possible. You held space for this dream long before it was born, and for that, I am eternally grateful.To my cherished friends and mentors—your wisdom has been a compass and your presence a blessing. Thank you for sharing your truths, encouraging my voice, and inspiring the spiritual insights woven throughout these pages.

A special thanks to Notion Press, whose support and editorial vision helped shape this book into the soulful offering it is today. Your belief in my message has been both humbling and empowering.

And finally, to you, dear reader—thank you for opening your heart to this journey. This book is not just mine; it is yours. May its words meet you exactly where you are, and gently guide you toward the peace, clarity, and sacred balance your soul seeks.

With infinite love and reverence,
Aashima, God's Child

# Prologue

There is a quiet voice within each of us, calling us to something deeper, something more meaningful. This voice speaks in moments of stillness, in moments when we pause long enough to listen. It reminds us that beyond the noise of our busy lives, beyond the demands of the world, there is a place of peace, wisdom, and connection—a place where we can truly be ourselves.

For many years, I tried to ignore that voice. I thought that in order to succeed, I had to keep moving forward, to push harder, to accomplish more. But the more I focused on the outer world, the more I felt disconnected from myself. It was only when I began to listen to that quiet inner voice that I found the balance I was searching for.

This book is my way of sharing that journey with you. It's an invitation to slow down, to turn inward, and to discover the beauty of a life lived in harmony with both the spiritual and the modern. Through these pages, I will share the lessons I have learned about finding peace amidst the chaos, about nurturing the soul in a world that often pulls us away from it.

As you embark on this journey with me, I encourage you to be open, to be curious, and most importantly, to be kind to yourself. There is no one "right" way to embrace spirituality in a modern world, but there are many ways to create balance, joy, and fulfillment in your life.

This book is my humble offering to you, a guide to living a soulful, balanced life in the midst of the ever-changing world around us.

# ONE

# AWAKENING IN THE MODERN WORLD: A CALL TO THE SOUL

Introduction: The Silent Craving for Something More

In the whirlwind of today's hyper-connected, always-on world, we often find ourselves sprinting through life—chasing deadlines, goals, and expectations—without stopping to ask why. Life becomes a checklist. Mornings blur into nights, weeks slip into months, and the heart, somewhere along the way, grows quieter beneath the noise.

Yet, amidst the buzzing of notifications and the endless to-do lists, there is a whisper. A subtle inner tug. A longing for depth, stillness, and connection. That whisper is not accidental. It is the call of your soul—inviting you to pause, breathe, and realign.

This chapter is not about retreating to a cave in the Himalayas or renouncing your ambitions. It is about awakening within the life you already live. It's about embracing spirituality not as an escape, but as an enhancement. You don't need to change your world—you need to change how you show up in it.

Let's begin this journey—right here, right now.

1.1 The Soul's Gentle Nudge in a Rushed Reality

We often wait for a crisis to reflect. Burnout. Heartbreak. Loss. But awakening doesn't always need to come from chaos. It can emerge in everyday moments—those rare pauses where we feel rather than perform.

Real-Life Moment: Arjun, the Finance Analyst

Arjun was a 29-year-old financial analyst known for being "the dependable one." Always on time. Always composed. One morning, as he sipped his coffee on a balcony before work, something strange happened—he felt the breeze. Noticed it. It wasn't groundbreaking, but it moved something within him.

"I realized I hadn't noticed anything in months," he later shared. That realization became his first step. Not quitting his job. Not moving to Bali. Just noticing the wind. From that day forward, he gave himself five tech-free minutes every morning. No phone. No thoughts about meetings. Just him and the present moment.

? Practice: The 5-Minute Stillness Reset

Every morning or evening, take 5 minutes of intentional silence. No music. No scrolling. Just sit. Breathe. Observe.

Ask: "How am I really feeling right now?"

Over time, this small practice becomes a sacred pause in your day—an invitation to connect.

Bonus Tip: Add a touch of nature if you can—sunlight, fresh air, a houseplant. The natural world has its own rhythm, and it gently reminds us of ours.

1.2 Awakening is for Everyone (Yes, Even You)

Many people think spirituality is for yogis, saints, or people with time. But awakening isn't about having time. It's about choosing moments. Spirituality isn't just prayer—it's awareness. It's reflection. It's being present as you wash the dishes or walk your dog.

Relatable Story: Sneha, the Startup Warrior

Sneha was building a startup. Her days were chaos—pitches, meetings, investors. Her nights? Mostly insomnia. After a panic attack in a restroom during a product demo, she began therapy and was encouraged to adopt "micro-mindfulness." Not yoga. Not journaling. Just breathing deeply for 3 minutes before entering a meeting room.

A few weeks later, she wasn't "zen," but she was different. More grounded. Less reactive. And for the first time in years, in touch with herself.

? Practice: The 3x3 Micro-Mindfulness

Three times a day, stop for 3 deep breaths. Say mentally: "I am here. I am enough. I am aware."

Try it before work, during lunch, and before sleep. Let awareness anchor your routine.

? Realization Exercise: Watch Without Judgment

Spend 10 minutes observing your thoughts. Imagine they're clouds passing in the sky.

Don't resist. Don't label. Just notice.

This builds the muscle of awareness—the root of spiritual awakening.

1.3 Awakening vs. Escaping

Let's be clear: awakening is not about running away from responsibility. It's about bringing your soul into those responsibilities. It's about shifting from doing to being—even while doing.

Practical Thought: You don't have to choose between ambition and peace. You can carry both.

Whether you're a CEO, a teacher, a student, or a parent—you don't have to abandon your life to embrace your soul. You just have to invite it in.

? Journal Prompt: Where am I feeling disconnected in life right now? What is one thing I can do differently this week to reconnect?

Power Quote:

"You can be grounded in your spirit while reaching for the stars. The roots and the wings—they both belong to you."

1.4 Daily Practices for the Modern Seeker

Here are some gentle, beginner-friendly practices you can integrate—even with a packed schedule:

1.4.1 Morning Soul Check-In (Time Needed: 3–5 Minutes)

Upon waking, sit up in bed and take three breaths.

Ask: "What energy do I want to carry today?"

Choose a word for the day: peace, clarity, strength, joy.

1.4.2 Digital Detox Hour (Choose any 60 minutes)

Choose an hour every day (even if split) where you're off screens.

Use that time to walk, read, stretch, or just be.

This rewires your brain and gives your soul space to breathe.

1.4.3 Gratitude Before Sleep (Time Needed: 2–3 Minutes)

Before sleeping, recall three things you're grateful for from the day.

This rewires your mind to find peace, not pressure, in your daily life.

1.4.4 The Sacred Commute

Turn your commute into a mindful experience.

Listen to soulful music, breathe deeply at red lights, or simply look outside with awareness.

Let the mundane become magical.

1.4.5 Soulful Sundays

Dedicate 30 minutes each Sunday to a soulful practice: reading an inspiring book, writing, nature walk, or just silence.

This becomes your weekly spiritual recharge.

1.5 The Transformative Power of Self-Compassion

Awakening is not about perfection. It's about progress. Often, we push ourselves to the brink, believing that doing more and pushing harder will lead to satisfaction. But awakening begins when we learn to be kinder to ourselves.

Story of Self-Compassion: Priya, the Overwhelmed Mother

Priya was a mother of two young children and a full-time marketing professional. She struggled with guilt—about not being "enough" for her children or at work. But one evening, after hearing a podcast on self-compassion, she had a breakthrough. She realized that her constant self-criticism only kept her disconnected from herself and her loved ones.

"I'm learning to treat myself like I would treat a friend," she explained. "With kindness, not judgment." That change in perspective was subtle but profound.

? Practice: The Compassionate Pause

When you feel overwhelmed, pause and ask: "What would I say to a friend who feels this way?"

Instead of judgment, offer yourself understanding. Acknowledge your efforts, no matter how small.

Bonus Insight: Self-compassion isn't about self-indulgence; it's about nurturing yourself to be the best version of you.

1.6 The Disconnect Between the Inner and Outer World

In today's society, there is often a disconnect between our inner and outer worlds. We are conditioned to prioritize external achievements—career success, financial stability, social status—over our inner well-being. We measure success by how much we can accomplish, but often neglect to ask ourselves whether we are truly fulfilled.

Real-Life Example: Neha, the High-Powered Executive

Neha, a high-powered CEO, had the world at her feet. But despite the prestige and wealth, she felt a deep emptiness inside. One day, during a solo retreat in the mountains, she took a walk in the forest. For the first time in years, she wasn't "performing" for anyone—she was simply being.

That moment of stillness was her awakening. She realized that success wasn't external—it was about internal alignment.

? Practice: Redefine Success

Ask yourself: What does true success look like for me?

It's not about how much you do. It's about how much you are in harmony with yourself.

1.7 When the Call Comes, Answer Softly

Awakening often begins with a whisper. A moment. A question that won't go away. Don't wait for burnout or breakdowns. You can start now—with small pauses, honest reflection, and conscious presence.

Your soul is not asking you to change everything overnight. It's asking you to remember who you are beneath all that you do.

List of Subtle Soul Calls:

A sudden craving for nature

A sense of emptiness after a busy day

A question that keeps returning

A tear that falls without reason

A smile that comes from nowhere

Each is a door. Walk through it.

Conclusion: The Journey Has Already Begun

If you've read this far, you've already taken your first step.

This chapter isn't just a collection of stories and practices—it's a mirror. A reminder. A hand on your shoulder whispering, you are more than your roles. You are a soul with a voice.

You don't have to run away to reconnect. You simply have to stop, breathe, and listen.

So here's your invitation:

? Create space.

? Be kind to yourself.

? Say yes to your soul's call—one small moment at a time.

Closing Affirmation: "In the midst of my busy life, I choose moments of stillness. I am awakening. I am remembering. I am home within myself."

The awakening has already begun. And it begins right here, right now—with you.

# TWO

# BALANCING MATERIAL SUCCESS AND SPIRITUAL FULFILLMENT

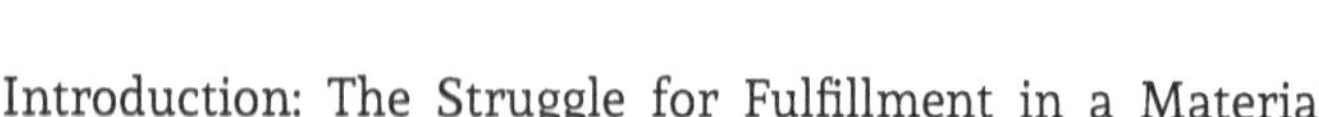

Introduction: The Struggle for Fulfillment in a Material World

In today's world, it often feels like the pursuit of material success is the only path to happiness. Whether it's securing a high-paying job, gaining financial stability, or achieving professional accolades, these external achievements are seen as milestones to be celebrated. But as we collect trophies of success, we often find ourselves yearning for something deeper—a sense of purpose, inner peace, and a spiritual connection that transcends the material.

We live in a world where external validation—like promotions, salaries, and accolades—defines success. Yet, true fulfillment doesn't lie solely in what is visible or measurable. It comes from within. In this chapter, we will explore how to find a balance between pursuing material success and nurturing spiritual fulfillment. We'll also share real-life examples, offering practical steps to help you live a more harmonious and balanced life.

2.1 The Material World: A Necessary Pursuit

Achieving material success is not inherently wrong. It's essential for creating a comfortable life, supporting your loved ones, and enjoying the pleasures this world offers. But focusing solely on material achievements can often leave us feeling disconnected from who we truly are. The key is to pursue material success with mindfulness, ensuring it complements your inner life, rather than overshadowing it.

Example of Riya's Journey (Corporate Story): Riya, a software engineer in a fast-paced startup, was driven by the desire to climb the corporate ladder. Every promotion was a marker of success, but after a few years, Riya noticed a deep sense of emptiness creeping in. "I realized that while I was succeeding at work, I was neglecting my emotional and spiritual well-being," she shared. Riya took a step back, reevaluated her priorities, and began integrating mindfulness practices into her daily routine. She started practicing gratitude before bed and engaging in short meditation sessions during breaks. Slowly, her achievements began to feel more fulfilling as they aligned with her inner values.

Example of Aarti (Retail Worker): Aarti, a shop assistant in a local grocery store, wasn't aiming for a corner office. She just wanted to make ends meet and provide for her children. However, after years of long hours and minimal personal time, she felt drained and disconnected. One day, a regular customer noticed Aarti's exhaustion and suggested, "Why not take a moment for yourself each day? Even ten minutes of quiet could help." Aarti began setting aside a few minutes before her shifts to pray and reflect. This simple practice brought her peace and clarity, making her work feel more meaningful. She realized that taking care of her spiritual health improved her interactions with customers and her overall well-being.

Suggested Practice:

Mindful Success: While working towards your goals, take time to reflect on why these goals matter to you. Ask yourself, "Does this bring me joy?" or "How does this align with my core values?" Set aside moments during the week to practice gratitude for what you've achieved, and ensure your pursuits align with your authentic self.

2.2 The Spiritual World: A Deep Connection

Material success is tangible and measurable, but spiritual fulfillment is often less visible and harder to quantify. Yet, true peace and contentment come from nurturing the soul—something that can't be bought or achieved by external means. In this section, we explore the importance of spiritual fulfillment in achieving lasting peace.

Story of Amit's Realization (Entrepreneur): Amit, a successful entrepreneur, was driven by ambition. His company was thriving, but he often found himself overwhelmed by constant pressure. One day, during a quiet trip to the mountains, Amit decided to disconnect from technology and spend time in nature. There, sitting by a river, something profound happened. "I realized that all the success in the world couldn't replace the peace I felt just being present," he reflected. Amit started taking regular "spiritual breaks"—moments to step away from work and reconnect with nature. Over time, this practice helped him return to his business with renewed focus and a deeper sense of purpose.

Example of Neelam (Housewife): Neelam, a homemaker, had always put the needs of her family first. She dedicated herself entirely to her children and husband, but as the years passed, she began to feel drained and unfulfilled. One evening, she attended a local temple gathering where the priest spoke about finding peace through spiritual practice. Neelam felt inspired and started taking short breaks in the day to meditate and connect with her faith. Gradually, she felt a shift—not just in her sense of peace, but in her ability to care for her family with greater love and patience.

Suggested Practice:

Nature as a Healer: Spend time in nature regularly, whether it's a walk in the park or a weekend hike. Nature has a calming effect that helps us reconnect with our inner self and find peace amidst the chaos of daily life.

2.3 Integrating the Two Worlds

The real challenge lies in integration—how do we live in a material world that prioritizes external success while nurturing our spiritual selves? The answer is not to reject material pursuits, but to find a way to blend both worlds seamlessly.

Example of Kiran's Integration (Corporate Professional): Kiran, a marketing professional, used to feel torn between her corporate career and her love for yoga and meditation. She either focused entirely on her work or immersed herself completely in spiritual practices. Over time, she realized that balance wasn't about choosing one over the other but about integrating both into her life. Kiran started her day with meditation and journaling, creating space for reflection before diving into her work. This morning ritual grounded her, and by the time she reached the office, she felt centered and energized.

Story of Ramesh (Teacher): Ramesh, a schoolteacher, had always been passionate about teaching, but he also yearned for spiritual peace. He started incorporating mindfulness into his daily routine—before going to school, he would spend ten minutes in quiet reflection. He also began using moments during the school day—like grading papers or waiting for the bell—to pause, take deep breaths, and align himself spiritually. Over time, Ramesh noticed that his energy and patience for his students increased, and he felt more connected to the essence of his work.

Suggested Practices:

Morning Ritual: Begin your day with a short spiritual practice, such as meditation, yoga, or journaling. This will help set a peaceful tone for the day and ensure you stay connected with your inner self, no matter what challenges arise.

Midday Pause: Take a few minutes during the day to pause and reconnect. Whether it's a deep breath, a quick walk, or a mindful coffee break, these moments can help you maintain balance and prevent burnout.

2.4 Overcoming the Guilt of Material Desires

Many people feel guilty about pursuing material success, especially when they are on a spiritual path. It's important to recognize that material desires are not inherently bad. As spiritual beings having a human experience, we are meant to engage with the material world in a way that doesn't detract from our spiritual growth.

Story of Meera's Dilemma (Social Worker): Meera, a social worker, dedicated her life to helping others, often sacrificing her personal needs for the sake of her work.

However, she began feeling guilty about her desire for financial stability and the comforts it could bring. It wasn't until a conversation with her mentor that she had a breakthrough. "My mentor reminded me that material desires are not wrong," Meera said. "You can enjoy the material world while staying grounded in your spiritual practice." This realization allowed Meera to embrace both her professional goals and her spiritual growth.

Example of Sandeep (Blue-Collar Worker): Sandeep, a mechanic, spent his life working long hours to provide for his family. However, he always struggled with feeling like he wasn't "spiritual enough" because of his material pursuits. One evening, after a long day at work, he attended a community meditation session. The teacher explained that material desires could coexist with spiritual fulfillment if approached with mindfulness. "The work you do feeds your family," the teacher said. "And in doing so, you are serving a higher purpose." This insight helped Sandeep release the guilt he had been carrying.

Example of Ananya (Job Seeker): Ananya, a recent graduate, was struggling to find a stable job. She felt pressured to succeed, both financially and professionally. She attended several interviews, but the constant rejection left her feeling anxious and disconnected from her purpose. During a conversation with a close friend, she admitted that she was feeling spiritually drained. Her friend encouraged her to practice gratitude daily and to focus on her personal growth during her job search. Ananya began incorporating daily meditation and journaling into her routine. She realized that by focusing on her personal well-being and spiritual growth, she attracted opportunities that aligned better with her values, ultimately leading her to a job that brought both stability and fulfillment.

Suggested Practice:

Release Guilt: Recognize that material desires and spiritual fulfillment can coexist. Write down your material goals and reflect on how they contribute to your overall well-being. This exercise can help you embrace both sides of your life without guilt.

2.5 Practical Steps to Achieve Balance

Achieving balance between material success and spiritual fulfillment is an ongoing process, but it's a journey worth embarking on. Here are a few practical steps you can take:

Set Intentions: At the start of each week, set both material and spiritual goals. For example, one goal might be to complete a work project, while another might be to spend time in meditation or prayer.

Create Boundaries: Ensure that your pursuit of material success doesn't dominate your life. Set clear boundaries between work and personal time, and make space for reflection and spiritual connection.

Find Meaning in Your Work: Whether you're a teacher, an engineer, or a stay-at-home parent, you can bring spiritual values into your work by practicing compassion, integrity, and mindfulness in all your interactions.

Example from Personal Experience: When I started writing this book, I found myself juggling the demands of life with my desire to stay spiritually grounded. Through intentional practices, such as setting weekly goals and creating boundaries, I learned that my spiritual journey enhanced my work, and my work benefited from my spiritual perspective. The balance wasn't perfect, but it was meaningful.

Conclusion: The Dance of Life

Balancing material success with spiritual fulfillment is an ongoing dance. Some days, you may feel more connected to the material world, and other days, you may be deeply connected to your spiritual self. The key is to remain mindful of both and create a harmonious relationship between them.

By aligning our actions with our values and creating space for spiritual practices, we can achieve a life that is both successful and deeply fulfilling—one that nurtures not just our external achievements but also our internal peace.

# THREE

# THE POWER OF MINDFULNESS IN EVERYDAY LIFE

Introduction: Finding Stillness in the Storm

In today's world, it feels like we're always on the go. Between work deadlines, family responsibilities, social media notifications, and endless to-do lists, it's no wonder many of us feel overwhelmed. Life can seem like a blur, where moments pass by in a rush, and we often don't take the time to really live them. We're so focused on what's coming next that we forget to enjoy what's happening right now.

Mindfulness is a simple yet powerful way to reconnect with the present moment and regain control over our lives. It's not about meditation retreats or finding hours of free time to sit still—it's about being fully present in the small moments of daily life, no matter how hectic or mundane they may seem. The beauty of mindfulness is that it's accessible to everyone, no matter how busy your schedule or chaotic your life might be.

This chapter will show you how mindfulness can fit into your daily routine and help you manage stress, increase focus, and improve your overall well-being. The best part? You can start right now, in whatever moment you find yourself.

3.1 What is Mindfulness?

Mindfulness is about paying attention to what's happening right now, without judgment. It's being fully engaged in whatever task or moment you're experiencing, whether that's a conversation, a cup of coffee, or a busy workday. Instead of being lost in your thoughts about the past or future, mindfulness brings you back to the present.

You don't have to go to a special class or meditate for an hour every day to practice mindfulness. It's about making a conscious effort to engage with your surroundings, thoughts, and emotions, without letting them control you.

Example of Nisha's Mindful Mornings: Nisha was always in a rush. As a lawyer with a demanding job, her mornings were a whirlwind of rushing to get dressed, grabbing a quick breakfast, and diving into work emails. She never had time to just breathe. After learning about mindfulness, Nisha decided to try a new habit: she woke up 10 minutes earlier to sit quietly and focus on her breath before diving into the chaos of the day.

The first few days felt odd, but soon Nisha noticed a shift. Her mornings felt less rushed, and she felt more grounded and calm when starting her day. What started as just a few minutes of breathwork grew into a powerful habit that helped her manage stress throughout the day.

Relatable Tip: Try setting your alarm 10 minutes earlier tomorrow. Use that time to simply focus on your breath, or stretch, or even just enjoy the feeling of the sun on your face. You'd be surprised at how such a small change can set the tone for your entire day.

3.2 The Benefits of Mindfulness

Mindfulness has far-reaching benefits. It can help you reduce stress, improve your emotional health, increase focus, and even boost your immune system. When we're constantly reacting to external pressures, our minds become cluttered. Mindfulness helps us sort through the noise and regain a sense of control.

Example of Karan's Transformation: Karan worked long hours at a tech firm, managing deadlines and teams. His work was stressful, and by the end of the day, he felt like a zombie—emotionally drained and disconnected. It wasn't until he started practicing mindfulness that things began to change. Whenever he felt the tension building up, Karan paused, took a few deep breaths, and simply observed his feelings without reacting.

Instead of snapping at his coworkers or stressing over the next deadline, Karan began to approach each task with a calmer mindset. His stress levels decreased, and his work performance improved. Mindfulness didn't just change his workday—it changed his life.

Mindfulness Tip: Whenever you feel stress creeping in, try this simple strategy: stop, take five deep breaths, and notice how your body feels. This break will help you reset your mind and keep stress at bay.

3.3 Everyday Mindfulness Practices

The best part about mindfulness is that you don't need special equipment, a meditation cushion, or hours of free time to practice. It can be incorporated into your daily routine, no matter how busy or stressful life may seem.

Mindful Eating: We've all been there—eating in front of the TV, at our desks, or while scrolling through our phones.

We eat, but we don't really taste our food. Mindful eating invites us to slow down and pay attention to the entire eating experience. Instead of rushing through meals, take a moment to appreciate the colors, textures, and flavors of your food. It can make even the simplest meal feel special.

Example of Rhea's Dinner Table Revolution: Rhea, a busy mom with three kids, was always multitasking during mealtimes. She would serve dinner while answering emails, sorting through laundry, or planning the next day. But she knew that mealtime should be a time to reconnect with her family. So, she decided to make a change. No phones, no distractions—just the family sitting together, sharing their day and enjoying the food in front of them.

At first, her kids were skeptical, but soon they began to look forward to these moments of connection. Mealtimes became less about just eating and more about being present with each other. It wasn't about perfecting every meal, but about making the moment feel more fulfilling and connected.

Mindfulness Tip: Next time you sit down to eat, turn off your phone, focus on the texture and taste of your food, and savor each bite. You'll find that your meals become more enjoyable and your relationship with food more meaningful.

Mindful Walking: Mindful walking is a great way to bring mindfulness into your day without having to set aside extra time. Whether it's a quick walk to the store or a longer stroll in the park, take a moment to focus on your surroundings. Pay attention to the feeling of your feet hitting the ground, the sounds around you, and your breath.

Example of Aarav's Office Walks: Aarav, an HR executive, was constantly stressed by his workload and long office hours. To break the cycle, he decided to incorporate mindful walking into his day. Instead of checking his phone or mentally preparing for his next task, Aarav focused on the simple act of walking—the rhythm of his steps, the feeling of the air on his face, and the sounds of the city around him. These brief moments of mindfulness allowed him to recharge and return to work with a clearer mind.

Mindfulness Tip: Take a few minutes today to walk mindfully. Whether it's on your way to work, the grocery store, or around your neighborhood, focus on your steps and the world around you.

3.4 The Role of Mindfulness in Relationships

Mindfulness is not just about how we interact with ourselves—it also transforms how we engage with others. By being present and truly listening, we can deepen our relationships and avoid misunderstandings.

Mindful Listening: How often are we really listening when someone is talking? In conversations, we're often thinking about our response, distracted by our phones, or simply waiting for our turn to speak. Mindful listening is about being fully present with the other person, listening without judgment or interruption.

Example of Meera and Her Daughter: Meera, a working mom, realized that she wasn't really listening to her teenage daughter, Simran. While Simran would talk about her day, Meera's mind would wander to work or chores. After practicing mindful listening, Meera made an effort to be fully present when Simran spoke. She stopped multitasking and gave her daughter her undivided attention.

Soon, Simran began opening up more, and their bond grew stronger. Meera realized that by simply listening mindfully, she had not only improved her relationship with Simran but also created a space for deeper, more meaningful conversations.

Mindfulness Tip: Try to listen without planning your response. Focus on the speaker's words and emotions, and you'll find that conversations become richer and more fulfilling.

Conclusion: The Path to Presence and Fulfillment

Mindfulness doesn't require grand gestures or hours of free time. It's about being present with your life as it is, right now. By practicing mindfulness in small, everyday moments—whether it's eating, walking, or listening—we can reduce stress, enhance our relationships, and find greater peace.

Life is busy, and it's easy to get caught up in the hustle and bustle. But by cultivating mindfulness, we can break free from the autopilot mode we often operate in and begin to truly live each moment. With every breath, every step, and every conversation, we have the power to be more present, more aware, and more connected.

So, what's stopping you from starting right now? Whether it's a quiet moment with your morning coffee or a walk after dinner, mindfulness is always available to you. Start small, and watch how it transforms your life, one moment at a time.

# FOUR

## FINDING PEACE IN THE CHAOS: THE POWER OF PAUSE

Introduction: The Silent Revolution Within

In today's fast-paced world, we often feel as though we're constantly running on a treadmill—moving, yet never really going anywhere. From early morning emails to late-night notifications, the constant demands of life keep us in motion, often at the expense of our well-being. But amidst the frenzy, there's a secret weapon that can bring us balance: stillness.

Stillness isn't about stepping away from life; it's about finding peace within it. It's not the absence of activity but the presence of mind—the ability to pause, breathe, and reconnect with ourselves, even in the busiest moments. In this chapter, we'll explore the power of pause and how it can help us regain our focus, reduce stress, and improve our mental clarity.

As we dive deeper, we'll discover real techniques, insightful quotes, and actionable steps to help you bring stillness into your life, making it easier to navigate the chaos and find peace.

4.1 The Power of Pausing: Why We Need Stillness More Than Ever

In a world that values hustle and productivity, stillness can feel counterintuitive. But what if slowing down was actually the key to moving forward?

Did you know? Research has shown that taking regular breaks throughout the day can significantly improve productivity and creativity. According to a study from the University of Illinois, when we take time to step away from work, our brains re-energize and boost performance.

This isn't just about resting physically—stillness allows us to rest mentally, providing the clarity we need to move forward. It's in these quiet moments that we can hear our inner voice and gain the insights that propel us toward our goals.

Quote:
"In the silence of the pause, we find the answers we are searching for." — Unknown

Example of Nisha's Realization of the Need for Pause: Nisha, a busy corporate executive and mother of two, felt overwhelmed by her packed schedule. She was constantly multitasking and moving from one responsibility to the next. One weekend, feeling drained, she decided to spend a few hours with her family, without checking her emails or social media. That simple act of pausing, of being present with her loved ones, made her realize how much she had been missing out on life's precious moments. From then on, Nisha started setting boundaries on her time, carving out small moments to reconnect with herself.

How to Implement:

Create Your Daily "Pause" Time: Set a specific time each day (even if it's just 10 minutes) where you step away from your tasks. Use this time for a mindful activity—meditation, a nature walk, or simply sitting in silence. This helps reset your mind and recharge your energy.

Use a Timer: Start with just 5 minutes of pause time and gradually increase it. Set an alarm or use a timer to remind yourself to take a break.

4.2 Facing the Fear of Stillness: Why We Distract Ourselves

Stillness can be intimidating because it often forces us to face uncomfortable thoughts and emotions. In a world full of distractions, it's easier to reach for our phones, turn on the TV, or fill our time with busywork rather than sit with our inner feelings. However, avoiding stillness often means avoiding self-awareness.

Did you know? Research has shown that many people experience "mind-wandering" when they're forced to be still. This mind-wandering is a sign that we are not used to being present with ourselves. However, psychologists suggest that mind-wandering can be a helpful tool for creativity and problem-solving if we allow ourselves to process it in a healthy way.

Quote:

"Stillness is not about avoiding the world. It's about seeing it more clearly." — Unknown

Example of Sanjay's Battle with His Inner Self: Sanjay, an entrepreneur, constantly found himself busy with work to avoid confronting his personal struggles. His anxiety about his business and future prevented him from slowing down. One evening, he decided to try sitting in silence. At first, his mind raced with worries, but as he continued practicing stillness daily, he found that his anxiety started to lessen, and he could think more clearly about his goals.

How to Implement:

Create a "Discomfort Zone": Choose one time a day to sit in stillness and allow yourself to feel whatever emotions arise. Whether you feel anxious, bored, or uneasy, sit with those feelings instead of running from them. This exercise helps build emotional resilience.

Journaling: After your stillness session, write down the thoughts that came up. Journaling helps process emotions and gain clarity.

4.3 Stillness Isn't Silence: How to Find Calm in Everyday Activities

Stillness doesn't always require complete silence or isolation. For some, stillness is found in activities that require full attention and presence. This could be anything from cooking a meal to gardening or listening to music. The goal is to engage fully in the present moment, allowing yourself to disconnect from the chaos and reconnect with yourself.

Did you know? Studies suggest that engaging in creative activities like cooking, painting, or gardening can reduce stress hormones and improve mood. This is known as "flow state," where time seems to disappear as you are absorbed in the task at hand.

Quote:

"When you are fully immersed in the present moment, you are practicing stillness in its truest form." — Unknown

Example of Sara's Creative Pause: Sara, a writer, often struggled to find peace amidst deadlines. One weekend, she decided to return to painting, a hobby she had abandoned for years. As she picked up her paintbrush, her mind slowed down, and she found herself completely immersed in the act of creation. That simple activity became her form of stillness, helping her regain energy and focus.

How to Implement:

Find Your Creative Outlet: Identify an activity you enjoy that allows you to be fully immersed. It could be painting, cooking, or even solving puzzles. Set aside time for this activity at least once a week.

Mindful Practice: As you engage in this activity, focus solely on the task at hand. Notice every detail—colors, textures, smells, or sounds. This mindfulness helps you stay grounded in the present moment.

4.4 Simple Ways to Cultivate Stillness Every Day

Stillness isn't something you have to schedule an hour for. It's about finding small pockets of peace throughout the day. Here are some detailed techniques to help you cultivate stillness:

1. Mindful Breathing (The 4-7-8 Technique)

Take five minutes every morning or night to practice mindful breathing. This technique helps calm the nervous system and centers the mind.

How to do it:

Inhale through your nose for a count of 4.

Hold your breath for a count of 7.

Exhale through your mouth for a count of 8.

Repeat the cycle 3-4 times.

Focus on the rhythm of your breath, allowing any thoughts to pass by without attachment.

2. Unplug and Unwind

Take regular breaks from your phone, computer, or TV. The digital world is a major source of stress and distraction. Even a 30-minute break can make a huge difference.

How to do it:

Set a timer for 30 minutes each day to be completely screen-free. Use this time to meditate, walk, or read a book.

Use apps like "Forest" to encourage digital detox and help you stay off your phone.

3. Nature Walks

Spending time in nature is one of the most effective ways to experience stillness. It offers natural quiet and the opportunity to connect with the world around you.

How to do it:

Take a walk in a park or by the beach.

Leave your phone behind, or keep it on airplane mode.

Engage all your senses—notice the colors, smells, and sounds of nature. Let it ground you.

4.5 Stillness and Connection: How It Deepens Our Relationships

Stillness doesn't only improve your personal well-being—it can enhance your relationships too. When we bring stillness into our interactions with others, we listen more attentively and communicate more thoughtfully.

Example of Ramesh's Relationship with His Partner: Ramesh, a busy entrepreneur, often found himself distracted during conversations with his partner. After learning about the importance of stillness, he made a conscious effort to listen without interrupting, putting his phone away during their discussions. Over time, this small shift brought them closer, and their conversations became more meaningful.

How to Implement:

Mindful Listening: In conversations, focus on truly hearing the other person. Don't interrupt or think about your response while they speak. Simply listen, fully engaged in the moment.

Ask Open-Ended Questions: Instead of rushing to give advice or solutions, ask questions that encourage deeper conversation. This fosters connection and shows genuine care.

Conclusion: The Peaceful Pause We All Deserve

In a world that constantly demands more of us, stillness offers a sanctuary—a moment to pause, breathe, and reconnect with our true selves. By incorporating small moments of stillness into our daily routines, we don't just find relief from stress; we also find clarity, creativity, and a deeper sense of connection with the world around us.

Stillness doesn't require perfection or grand gestures; it's about giving ourselves permission to slow down and be present, even in the middle of life's chaos. Whether through mindful breathing, taking a walk, or simply listening with our full attention, we can all find peace in the pauses.

# FIVE

# THE POWER OF MINDFUL CONNECTION

Introduction: In an age where notifications, scrolling, and instant messaging dominate our lives, it's deeply ironic that many of us feel more isolated than ever. Despite being surrounded by digital connections, we often long for something deeper—authentic human relationships grounded in presence and empathy. This chapter explores the transformative power of mindful connection: how being present, actively listening, and practicing empathy can reshape the way we connect with others and ourselves.

Mindful connection is about being truly available in a moment, offering our full attention, and engaging with authenticity. It doesn't require long hours or grand gestures—it requires intention. Whether it's through conversations with friends, colleagues, or partners, the practices shared in this chapter will help you forge deeper, more fulfilling relationships.

5.1 The Difference Between Being Connected and Truly Connecting

Modern tools like social media and messaging apps have revolutionized communication, yet they often foster superficial interactions. We might be constantly in touch, but rarely in tune.

Example: Sia and Priya Sia, a marketing manager, had stayed connected with her friend Priya via social media—likes, comments, and birthday messages. But it felt empty. Inspired by an article on mindful connection, Sia called Priya. She turned off distractions, sat in a quiet room, and practiced active listening—no multitasking, no quick replies. The conversation flowed deeply, and they shared personal stories. It rekindled a lost intimacy. Sia realized that mindful presence made her feel more nourished than hundreds of online interactions ever did.

Technique: Intentional Presence

Before engaging with someone, pause and take three deep breaths.

Silence or put away your phone.

Make eye contact and set an intention to listen fully.

Respond only after the other person finishes.

5.2 The Art of Active Listening

We often listen to reply, not to understand. True listening is an act of compassion.

Example: Neha and Her Team Neha, a team leader, noticed her team was disengaged. She implemented a new strategy: she listened during meetings without interrupting, acknowledged emotions, and repeated what she heard to confirm understanding. Her team began opening up more. As they felt heard, their contributions grew meaningful, and collaboration improved.

Technique: The LISTEN Model

L – Look into their eyes and give nonverbal cues.

I – Inquire with open-ended questions.

S – Silence your inner voice.

T – Take notes mentally or on paper.

E – Empathize, validate feelings.

N – Nod or show understanding.

5.3 Mindful Communication in Personal Relationships

When emotions run high, we often speak from a place of defense rather than understanding. Mindful communication nurtures emotional intimacy.

Example: Vikram and Anjali Vikram and Anjali argued frequently. After attending a mindfulness workshop, they agreed to pause before reacting. During their next disagreement, they took deep breaths, let each other finish, and responded with calm reflection. Slowly, their communication shifted from combative to collaborative.

Technique: The 3-Second Pause

Before replying in a tense conversation, count to 3 silently.

Observe your body language.

Ask: "Am I responding or reacting?"

Actionable Steps:

Use "I" statements: "I feel..." instead of "You always..."

Reflect what you hear: "What I'm hearing is..."

Ask for clarity: "Can you help me understand...?"

5.4 Practicing Empathy in Connections

Empathy transforms relationships. It's the difference between offering solutions and offering support.

Example: Arjun and Meera Arjun noticed Meera, a team member, was overwhelmed. Instead of offering advice, he invited her to talk. He listened with compassion, validated her feelings, and simply said, "I hear you, and I'm here." That simple moment changed the dynamic—they built trust and connection.

Technique: Reflective Empathy

Mirror emotions: "You seem really frustrated."

Validate without fixing: "That makes sense. I'd feel the same."

Ask: "What would support look like right now?"

5.5 Cultivating Mindful Connection in the Workplace

Workplaces can either foster stress or connection. Mindfulness can shift cultures.

Example: Poonam's Meetings Poonam implemented a mindfulness practice at the start of each meeting—60 seconds of silence. Over time, her team became more present, patient, and productive. Conversations were more focused. Conflicts reduced. The culture shifted.

Technique: Mindful Meeting Minutes

Start meetings with 1 minute of silence.

Set a shared intention: "Let's listen openly today."

Use a talking stick or hand raise to reduce interruptions.

Reflection Exercises

Recall your last deep conversation. What made it feel meaningful?

Identify someone in your life you haven't truly "seen" lately. How can you reach out mindfully?

Reflect on a time you felt truly heard. How did it change you?

Journaling Prompts

Who in my life do I want to build a deeper connection with?

How can I bring more presence into my conversations?

What stops me from listening fully—and how can I change that?

Illustration Ideas

Digital vs Real Connection (Side-by-side contrast)

The LISTEN Model as a visual acronym

Heart-centered empathy map

Conclusion: The Gift of Connection Mindful connection isn't just a spiritual practice—it's a life-changing tool. It heals relationships, builds community, and brings deep fulfillment. By choosing presence over performance, empathy over efficiency, and depth over digitality, we reclaim what it means to be human.

In practicing these techniques daily, you not only transform your relationships—you transform yourself. You become the safe space where others feel seen, heard, and held. That's the true power of mindful connection.

Next Step: 5-Day Mindful Connection Challenge

Day 1: Call someone you usually text.

Day 2: Listen without interrupting.

Day 3: Thank someone meaningfully.

Day 4: Sit in silence with a loved one.

Day 5: Write a letter to someone you care about.

**Reflection Exercises**

? Reflection Exercise 1: Are You Truly Connecting?

Prompt:

Think about your last three conversations—were you truly present? Did you listen or just hear? Were you seeking to understand or simply to respond?

Action Step:

Write down the names of the three people you interacted with.

Rate your presence in each conversation from 1–10.

Reflect: What could you have done differently to show more empathy or presence?

? Reflection Exercise 2: The Empathy Mirror

Prompt:

Consider a recent moment when someone shared a

challenge with you. How did you respond? Was it advice, dismissal, or empathy?

Action Step:

Revisit that moment mentally.

Now, write a new response rooted in empathy.

Ask yourself: If I were in their shoes, how would I want someone to respond to me?

? Reflection Exercise 3: Screen or Soul?

Prompt:

Assess your digital communication habits. Are they helping you build meaningful relationships or fragmenting your attention?

Action Step:

For one full day, track how many digital conversations you have.

Of those, how many felt truly meaningful?

Try replacing one digital conversation with a voice call or face-to-face talk tomorrow. Record how it feels.

?? Journaling Prompts

Describe a moment when you felt deeply connected to someone. What made that moment meaningful?

Who in your life deserves more of your mindful presence? How can you start showing up for them better this week?

What emotional barriers prevent you from listening openly and without judgment? How can you gently work through them?

Write a letter (unsent) to someone with whom you've lost touch. What would you say if you could speak mindfully, from the heart?

What does "being present" look and feel like to you? Describe a space, mood, or habit that helps you anchor into the now.

? Illustration Ideas

"The Presence Scale" Visual – A thermometer-style graphic showing different levels of attention (Distracted → Multitasking → Listening → Deep Presence).

Empathy Circle Illustration – A heart-centered diagram showing:

Listen

Feel

Validate

Support

(These can be shown as overlapping petals of a flower of connection.)

Digital vs. Mindful Connection Split Image

Left side: Two people texting on their phones while sitting together.

Right side: The same people in deep conversation, eyes engaged, no phones.

Mindful Communication Flowchart

Trigger → Pause → Breathe → Listen → Acknowledge → Respond with Empathy

"Room for Silence" Visual – A cozy tea scene with two people sitting quietly, a quote below:

"Silence isn't the absence of communication, it's the space where hearts are heard."

? Bonus: Weekly Mindful Connection Challenge

Challenge: 5 Days of Deeper Connection

DayPracticeReflection

Day 1Call someone instead of textingHow did the conversation feel different?

Day 2Listen to someone without interruptingWhat did you learn about them? About yourself?

Day 3Share a personal story with someoneHow did that vulnerability feel?

Day 4Thank someone genuinelyHow did they respond?

Day 5Spend 10 minutes in silence with a loved oneWhat emotions surfaced?

Embrace this journey—your relationships and your heart will thank you.

# SIX

# The Intersection of Science and Spirituality – A New Perspective

In our fast-paced, hyper-connected modern world, we often see science and spirituality as opposing forces—like oil and water, never truly mixing. Science is grounded in evidence, experimentation, and logic. Spirituality, on the other hand, is rooted in intuition, faith, and inner experience. But what if this division isn't necessary? What if, instead, we began to see these two powerful disciplines as complementary perspectives offering a more complete picture of reality?

In this chapter, we'll take a simplified yet profound journey to understand how science and spirituality are converging. We'll explore how ancient spiritual wisdom aligns with modern scientific discoveries and how embracing both can help us live more meaningful, balanced, and enriched lives.

6.1 The Historical Divide Between Science and Spirituality

For centuries, science and spirituality have seemed like two roads diverging. The Enlightenment period in the 17th and 18th centuries emphasized rationality, skepticism, and proof. Anything that couldn't be measured or tested was dismissed as superstition. Spiritual traditions were sidelined as outdated or irrational.

However, if we look further back, we see a different story. Ancient Indian sages, Greek philosophers like Pythagoras and Plato, and even early Egyptian thinkers didn't separate science and spirituality. In fact, they saw them as deeply interconnected.

Ancient Indian Perspective: The Vedas, written thousands of years ago, contain references to astronomy, medicine (Ayurveda), and even atomic theory. Yet, these scientific explorations were never separated from spiritual practices like meditation, prayer, and mantra chanting.

Greek Thinkers: Plato believed that true knowledge came not only from the senses but also from contemplation—a spiritual process. His concept of the "realm of forms" mirrors the spiritual idea of a higher, unseen reality.

Albert Einstein's Insight: Einstein's quote, "Science without religion is lame, religion without science is blind," reflects his belief that science and spirituality are not enemies. While he didn't follow a traditional religion, he often spoke of a "cosmic religious feeling"—a deep reverence for the mysteries of the universe.

## 6.2 Quantum Physics: When Reality Becomes Mysterious

Quantum physics—the study of particles smaller than atoms—has revolutionized our understanding of the universe. It shows us a world where things don't always behave logically. Instead of being predictable, particles act like waves, exist in multiple states at once, and only settle into one position when observed. This mirrors spiritual teachings that emphasize the mysterious, interconnected nature of reality.

The Observer Effect: The famous double-slit experiment shows that particles behave differently when observed. When no one is watching, particles act like waves. But when observed, they act like solid matter. This raises a profound question: Does consciousness affect reality?

Spiritual Parallel: Eastern philosophies, such as Vedanta and Buddhism, have long taught that the mind creates or influences reality. "As you think, so you become," is not just a spiritual aphorism—it may now be backed by quantum science.

Example: Dr. Amit Goswami: In his book The Self-Aware Universe, physicist Amit Goswami explains how consciousness may be the foundation of everything. He argues that the universe isn't just material—it's conscious. This view aligns with spiritual teachings that describe the universe as an extension of divine or universal consciousness.

## 6.3 Everything Is Connected: The Holistic View

Modern science increasingly supports a view of reality that spiritual traditions have promoted for millennia: that everything is connected. Systems thinking, ecology, and integrative medicine show that we can't understand any part of life in isolation.

Biology: Systems biology looks at how every part of a living organism affects the whole. Genes, proteins, and cells don't operate in isolation. They're deeply interdependent, like instruments in an orchestra.

Ecology: Environmental science teaches us that humans, animals, plants, air, and water are all part of one system. When one piece suffers, the entire system is affected. Indigenous spiritual traditions, such as those of Native Americans and Australian Aboriginals, have taught this for generations.

Example: Fritjof Capra's "The Tao of Physics": Capra compared quantum physics with Taoist and Buddhist philosophies, showing that modern science and ancient wisdom describe the same reality in different languages. Both speak of unity, flow, and the interconnectedness of all things.

6.4 The Brain on Spirit: Neuroscience and Mystical States

Neuroscience—the study of the brain—is now exploring what happens when people engage in deep meditation, prayer, or spiritual practices. What once seemed unmeasurable is now being scanned, analyzed, and mapped.

The Default Mode Network (DMN): This part of the brain is associated with self-referential thoughts—worry, planning, ego. Regular meditation has been shown to reduce DMN activity, leading to reduced anxiety and increased presence.

Neuroplasticity: Studies reveal that spiritual practices can physically change the brain. With consistent meditation or prayer, people grow more grey matter in areas responsible for emotional regulation, empathy, and focus.

Example: Dr. Andrew Newberg: In his book How God Changes Your Brain, Newberg explains how spiritual practices affect neurological function. People in deep prayer or meditation often report a sense of losing their boundaries and merging with the universe—what mystics describe as "oneness." Brain scans show reduced activity in the parietal lobes, which helps explain this feeling.

6.5 Daily Life: How to Use Science and Spirituality Together

It's not just about theory—this intersection can improve your daily life. You don't need to choose between being rational and being spiritual. You can meditate and be logical. You can study scientific principles and practice gratitude.

Strategies for Integrating Both:

1. Practice Mindfulness Scientifically:

Use meditation apps like Headspace or Calm that are backed by science.

Try a 10-minute breathing exercise each morning. This improves focus and lowers stress, as shown by multiple neuroscience studies.

2. Eat and Live Holistically:

Follow integrative health practices that combine nutrition, exercise, and mindfulness.

Learn about Ayurveda or Traditional Chinese Medicine and see how they align with modern nutritional science.

3. Journal Your Insights:

Write daily reflections like: "What did I learn today that connects both logic and intuition?"

Track your mood and spiritual practices and see how they affect your energy and clarity.

4. Explore Nature Scientifically and Spiritually:

Learn about the ecosystem while hiking.

Practice "forest bathing" or mindful walking. Recognize your connection to every tree and bird, not just as a visitor, but as a part of nature.

Example: Steve Jobs' Life Philosophy Jobs studied Zen Buddhism and credited it for his focus and creativity. He combined intuition with innovation, helping to create not just products, but experiences. His approach shows how spiritual clarity can enhance scientific genius.

Reflection Exercises and Journaling Prompts

Reflection Exercises:

Sit quietly and observe your breath. Ask: "Where do my thoughts come from?"

Look up at the night sky. Ask: "What connects me to the stars?"

Journaling Prompts:

Describe a moment when you felt both logically clear and spiritually inspired.

How do you see science supporting your spiritual beliefs?

What scientific discoveries make you feel awe or wonder?

Conclusion: A Unified Path Forward

Science explains how the universe works. Spirituality helps us explore why it exists and how we relate to it. Together, they don't contradict—they complete.

We live in a time when this integration is not only possible but essential. By embracing both, we become more balanced, compassionate, and wise. We stop living in either/or and start living in both/and.

As Blaise Pascal once wrote, "The heart has its reasons of which reason knows nothing." But what if we could let the heart and reason walk hand in hand?

Let that be your new way of living—where truth meets trust, logic meets love, and science meets spirit.

6.6 Meaningful Practices for a Unified Life

Blending science and spirituality isn't just an idea—it's a lifestyle you can actively cultivate. Below are practices that help harmonize logic with intuition, evidence with experience, and data with divine presence. These are practical, grounded in research, yet deeply soul-nourishing.

1. The Morning Integration Ritual

Start your day with a practice that grounds you both scientifically and spiritually.

Scientific Side: Begin with 5 minutes of focused deep breathing. Inhale for 4 counts, hold for 4, exhale for 6. This activates the parasympathetic nervous system, reducing cortisol and enhancing focus (as shown in studies by Stanford neuroscientist Andrew Huberman).

Spiritual Side: Follow with 5 minutes of silent gratitude or prayer. Thank the universe, divine, or your higher self for another day. Speak from the heart.

? Example: Light a candle, sit quietly, and whisper: "Today, I am open to insight, grace, and action."

2. The Science-Spirit Journal

Keep a dedicated journal to track your experiences through both lenses.

Scientific Practice: Record your sleep hours, energy levels, mood, and food intake.

Spiritual Practice: Reflect on synchronicities, dreams, or intuitive nudges you felt that day.

? Prompt: "What did I experience today that felt meaningful beyond logic?"

? Bonus Insight: Over time, you may notice patterns—perhaps your intuition is strongest when you sleep well or eat certain foods. This is real-time integration of data and divine!

3. Energy Experiments (Inspired by Dr. Joe Dispenza)

Dr. Dispenza, a neuroscientist who healed his own spinal injury through meditation, teaches that focused thought + elevated emotion = transformation.

Practice:

Visualize a goal (e.g., healing, success, peace) while feeling elevated emotions like joy, gratitude, or love.

Do this for 10 minutes daily. MRI studies show increased coherence in the brain and heart when this is done consistently.

? Scientific Tie-In: HeartMath Institute research shows that when heart and brain are in sync, the body enters a state of harmony, known as "coherence." This enhances intuition and decision-making.

4. Forest Bathing with Awareness

"Shinrin-yoku" or forest bathing originated in Japan and is now validated by science.

Scientific Practice: A 30-minute walk in nature lowers blood pressure, boosts immunity, and reduces stress hormones.

Spiritual Practice: As you walk, silently say, "I am one with all that lives." Touch a tree, notice a bird's call, and breathe it all in—not just as sights and sounds, but sacred signs of connection.

? Real-Life Tip: Leave your phone behind. Walk slowly. Let your inner and outer worlds meet.

5. Mindful Tech Usage (Digital Spirituality)

In a hyper-connected world, spirituality can be practiced through mindful tech usage.

Scientific Awareness: Studies show frequent phone checking increases anxiety.

Spiritual Practice: Turn your device into a tool for presence. Set reminders like:

"Pause. Breathe. Be."

"What's the deeper message in this moment?"

? Meaningful Tip: Unfollow accounts that promote fear or ego. Follow those that elevate your consciousness.

6. Sacred Science Reading Hour

Dedicate an hour weekly to reading works that bridge science and spirituality.

Suggestions:

The Biology of Belief by Bruce Lipton

The Tao of Physics by Fritjof Capra

Becoming Supernatural by Dr. Joe Dispenza

The Seat of the Soul by Gary Zukav

? Reflection: After reading, write down one idea you can apply practically.

7. Monthly Science-Spirit Reflection Day

Take one day a month for deeper integration. This could be a Sunday retreat at home.

Sample Schedule:

Morning: Meditation + reading a scientific article on consciousness

Afternoon: Nature walk + journaling

Evening: Breathwork or mantra chanting + reflecting on what you've learned from both perspectives

? Journal Prompt: "What does my rational mind think about this? What does my intuitive heart feel about it?"

8. Energy Hygiene Practice

Just like physical hygiene, energetic hygiene helps you stay balanced.

Scientific Understanding: Emotions and stress are measurable in brain waves, heart rate, and hormonal responses.

Spiritual Tools:

Grounding: Walk barefoot on grass for 10 minutes.

Visualization: Imagine a white light cleansing your aura.

Sound: Listen to 432 Hz music, believed to align with natural vibration of the universe.

? Pro-Tip: Use apps like Insight Timer or YouTube for healing frequencies backed by studies in vibrational medicine.

9. Science-Spirituality Buddy Circle

Create a small group of friends or family who enjoy both logic and intuition. Meet monthly.

Discuss a new scientific discovery (e.g., quantum entanglement or brain plasticity).

Share personal spiritual experiences and how they relate.

Meditate together or explore a new practice.

? Conversation Starter: "Have you ever had a dream that came true? Could that be quantum possibility in action?"

Final Reflection: The Balanced Mind, the Expanded Soul

True wisdom lies not in choosing between science or spirituality, but in dancing with both. When we meditate, we're not abandoning logic—we're rebalancing the brain. When we study quantum theory, we're not rejecting intuition—we're decoding the divine.

? Remember:

Science shows us the how.

Spirituality shows us the why.

Together, they reveal the whole.

# SEVEN

## The Power of Present Moment – Embracing Mindfulness in Everyday Life

In the hustle and bustle of modern life, we often find ourselves constantly moving, planning, and worrying about the future or dwelling on the past. We rarely stop to experience the present moment—the here and now. This is where the practice of mindfulness becomes a life-changing tool. Mindfulness is the simple yet profound practice of being fully aware of what is happening in the present moment, without judgment or distraction.

But mindfulness is not just a technique—it's a way of being. It is an invitation to live with intention, to find meaning in the ordinary, and to discover the sacred in the mundane. This chapter will explore how we can all embrace mindfulness in our daily lives, regardless of our age, occupation, or circumstances—and how this simple shift in awareness can lead to a deeply fulfilling life.

7.1 Understanding Mindfulness: More Than a Trend

While mindfulness has been a hot topic in recent years—celebrated by CEOs, therapists, influencers, and wellness gurus—it is far more than a wellness trend. At its heart, mindfulness is about being fully awake to life. It invites us to notice what we often miss when we're on autopilot: the warmth of sunlight, the softness in someone's voice, the rhythm of our own breath.

Spiritual Root and Scientific Relevance: Ancient Buddhist texts define mindfulness (Sati) as the ability to maintain awareness of our body, feelings, and thoughts in the present moment. Interestingly, modern psychology now uses similar principles in mindfulness-based cognitive therapy (MBCT) to treat anxiety, depression, and emotional distress.

Example: When sipping a cup of tea, do you actually taste it—or is your mind already racing toward the next email or meeting? Mindfulness teaches us to slow down and experience each moment in its richness, instead of letting life pass us by in a blur.

7.2 Why Mindfulness Matters More Than Ever

In today's hyper-digital, always-on world, the mind is constantly overstimulated. Notifications, deadlines, social media comparison, and unending to-do lists have created what psychologists now call "continuous partial attention"—a state where we're never fully focused on anything, and our nervous system remains in low-level survival mode.

This is where mindfulness becomes a remedy, not just a practice.

Scientifically Proven Benefits:

Reduces cortisol (the stress hormone)

Enhances memory, attention, and emotional intelligence

Increases empathy and resilience

Boosts immune system and slows cellular aging (yes, really!)

Real-Life Example: Mindfulness in the Corporate World Top organizations like Google, Apple, and General Mills have integrated mindfulness programs into their culture. Google's "Search Inside Yourself" program teaches emotional intelligence through mindfulness, proving it's not just a spiritual tool—it's a productivity and leadership enhancer.

7.3 Deeper Daily Practices to Cultivate Mindfulness

Here's how mindfulness can be embedded seamlessly into your daily life—not as something extra to do, but as a more conscious way of doing what you're already doing.

Mindful Mornings: Start With Presence

Before reaching for your phone in the morning, take three conscious breaths. Feel your feet on the floor, stretch your body, notice how you feel. These 30 seconds set the tone for your entire day.

"The way you start your morning defines your momentum."

Mindful Transitions: The Power of the Pause

Between tasks, take a moment to reset your mind. Whether you're switching meetings or moving from work to home mode, pausing helps you arrive fully present in your next moment.

Micro-Practice: Close your eyes, inhale for 4 seconds, exhale for 6. Do this three times. Notice the shift.

Mindful Technology Use

We check our phones over 80 times a day—mostly unconsciously. Try setting intentions before each phone use. Ask: Why am I reaching for this? What do I hope to find?

Use your phone as a mindfulness tool:

Set reminders to breathe or pause every few hours.

Change your lock screen to a mindful mantra like "Be Here Now."

7.4 Healing Through Mindfulness: Emotional and Mental Wellness

Mindfulness isn't about avoiding emotions—it's about facing them with compassion.

Practice: R.A.I.N. for Emotional Clarity

A widely used mindfulness technique for dealing with difficult emotions:

R – Recognize the emotion

A – Allow it to be there

I – Investigate its cause or sensation

N – Nurture it with compassion

Example: You feel anxious before a difficult conversation. Instead of suppressing or overanalyzing, pause. Recognize the tightness in your chest. Allow the fear. Investigate the root—is it fear of rejection? Then nurture yourself: "It's okay to feel this way. I am safe."

7.5 Mindfulness in Relationships: Presence is the Greatest Gift

Mindfulness allows us to truly see and hear others. In a distracted world, being fully present with someone is rare—and powerful.

Practice: The 60-Second Connection

Next time you're talking to someone, give them your full attention for 60 seconds. No judgment. No advice. Just listen. Let silence be okay.

Example: In a world of fast replies and multitasking, your mindful presence can make someone feel deeply valued. For parents, partners, and friends—this is the most meaningful gift.

7.6 Mindfulness for Inner Peace in Challenging Times

Life won't always go smoothly. But mindfulness equips us to respond instead of react. When practiced regularly, it creates space between stimulus and response—a space filled with wisdom and calm.

Real-Life Story: Mindfulness During Grief

After losing a loved one, many people find comfort in mindfulness. Simply sitting with the breath or being present with tears—without judgment—helps process grief gently. Mindfulness doesn't take away the pain; it teaches us to sit beside it with love.

7.7 Creating a Mindful Environment

A mindful life is supported by a mindful space.

Declutter your room. A clear space equals a clear mind.

Light a candle or incense—smell anchors you to the now.

Add a gratitude board or small altar where you can pause and reflect.

Practice: Mindful Cleaning Even chores can be meditative. Feel the warmth of water, the texture of soap, the motion of your hands. Turn housework into a sacred act of self-care.

Reflection Practices and Journaling Prompts
Evening Reflections:
What moment today brought me peace or joy?
Was there a time I was fully present? How did it feel?

Morning Intentions:

How can I bring more awareness into today?

Who or what deserves my full attention today?

Weekly Journaling Prompts:

In what ways is mindfulness shifting how I see the world?

What distractions consistently pull me away from the present?

What's one thing I will do mindfully this week?

Conclusion: Presence is the Portal to Peace

Mindfulness is not about escaping life—it's about entering it more fully. It's not about being calm all the time—it's about being real, present, and awake to the full spectrum of human experience.

When we practice mindfulness, we awaken to the miracle of being alive. We stop existing on autopilot and begin to truly live.

In the words of Thich Nhat Hanh:

"The present moment is filled with joy and happiness. If you are attentive, you will see it."

So take this moment—this one, right here—and inhale it fully. Let the now be enough. Let it be sacred.

# EIGHT

## THE JOURNEY WITHIN – EMBRACING THE DIVINE CONNECTION

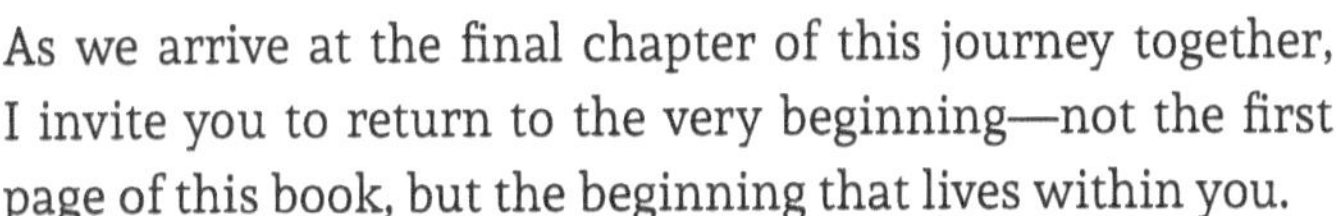

As we arrive at the final chapter of this journey together, I invite you to return to the very beginning—not the first page of this book, but the beginning that lives within you.

This book was never meant to be a manual or a doctrine. It is a mirror—a gentle invitation to see yourself as you truly are: whole, radiant, and profoundly connected to something greater. The true journey has always been about awakening the soul, embracing the sacred within the ordinary, and recognizing that the answers you seek do not lie outside you—they already live in your heart.

This is not the end.
This is your beginning.

8.1 The Essence of Your Inner Journey

We are taught to chase meaning in external milestones—degrees, job titles, applause, approval. But even after crossing the finish line, many still feel the void. Why? Because what your soul longs for is not success—it's connection.

The deeper purpose of your life is not to impress the world but to express your true self—freely, joyfully, and with reverence for the sacred essence that breathes through you.

"You are not a drop in the ocean. You are the entire ocean in a drop." – Rumi

Each moment of struggle, joy, loss, and revelation has been guiding you home. Not to a physical place, but to the sacred space of your own soul.

8.2 Divine in the Everyday: A Living Spirituality

Spirituality doesn't belong only in temples, ashrams, or mountaintops. It belongs at your dining table, in your inbox, your morning commute, your child's laughter, and your quiet tears.

The Divine is not a destination—it's a dimension of awareness.

Real-Life Spark: A woman once told me she found her deepest connection to God while standing barefoot in her garden, hands covered in soil, tears on her cheeks, whispering thank you to the sky. No mantras. No rituals. Just presence. That was her prayer.

When you bring sacred attention to any moment, it becomes holy.

You don't have to seek the Divine. You just have to see it. It's in your breath. It's in your becoming. It's you.

8.3 The Heartbeat of This Book

At its core, this journey has been about dissolving the illusion that we must choose between the material and the spiritual. You were never meant to choose—you were meant to integrate.

The real power lies in living both worlds simultaneously:

Being present at work and deeply connected to purpose.

Enjoying wealth, yet unattached to it.

Loving others fully, without losing yourself.

This integration is sacred alchemy—it's the soul dancing in the world without forgetting its rhythm.

"To live in the world and yet not be of it, to touch everything and yet remain rooted in the Self—that is the art of a modern mystic."

8.4 A Call to Embody Your Divine Self

You are not broken.

You are not behind.

You are not too late.

You are exactly where you are meant to be, blossoming in divine timing.

The lotus doesn't bloom in perfect water. It rises from the mud.

All the moments you thought were breaking you? They were awakening you. You are not here by accident. You are here to remember who you are—a soul on a sacred mission to bring light into a world that desperately needs your truth.

Let the past no longer be your prison, but your proof: you have survived, grown, and risen.

8.5 A Living Ritual – Claiming Your Inner Light

Let's mark this moment. You've read, reflected, evolved. Now it's time to claim it—not just mentally, but spiritually and energetically.

? Your Embodiment Ritual:

Sit in silence. Close your eyes and place one hand on your heart.

Whisper these words aloud or within:

"I am Divine. I am whole. I now walk with purpose, with love, and with the light of my soul. I am free."

Visualize golden light filling your body, from your crown to your toes.

Imagine your future self—calm, confident, joyful—walking beside you, smiling. That future self is already you.

Breathe in that truth. Anchor it in your being.

This is more than an ending—it's an energetic rebirth.

8.6 The Deeper Truth: This Is Just the Beginning

The destination is not enlightenment.

The destination is presence, truth, and sacred alignment with your soul.

When you live this way, even traffic becomes a temple. Even pain becomes poetry. Even silence becomes a song.

So what now?

Now you walk.

You walk forward—with courage in your heart and light in your steps. You trust yourself. You soften your judgments. You honor your needs. And you live—not just for the world's applause, but for your soul's joy.

Final Blessing: A Love Letter to Your Soul

Dear reader,

You are loved more than you know.

You are seen more deeply than you realize.

You are held by a force greater than any fear.

In your moments of doubt, return to this truth:

You are not alone. You never were.

Let this chapter be your reminder. Let this book be your sacred companion. But most importantly, let your life be the

altar where your spirit dances freely.
This is the journey within.
And you, beautiful soul, are ready.
With infinite love,
– Aashima (God's Child)
??? End of Book. Beginning of You. ???

# Closing Thoughts

As I close this final chapter, my heart is full—with gratitude, with reverence, and with hope.

This book was never meant to be just words on a page. It was meant to be a mirror, a companion, a spark—guiding you gently back home to yourself. If, along the way, you felt even one moment of awakening, one breath of stillness, one whisper of truth rising from within—you've already begun the transformation this journey was designed to inspire.

We live in a world that often asks us to be more, do more, chase more. But the real magic begins when you pause, look within, and realize: You were always enough.

May you walk forward not as someone searching for light—but as someone who carries it.

May you remember that spirituality is not about escaping the world, but about engaging with it—fully, bravely, and soulfully.

And may you always know this:

The Divine lives in you, walks with you, and speaks through you.

You are never alone. You are never lost. You are already home.

Thank you for allowing me to walk this path with you.

May your journey be radiant, purposeful, and full of love.

With all my heart,

– Aashima

(God's Child)

# About The Author

By profession, I am a Software Engineer — someone who finds beauty in logic, structure, and the ever-evolving world of technology. But beyond the codes and systems, my soul has always felt a deep connection with the Universe — a pull toward something greater, something eternal.

I am a seeker. A passionate spiritual orator, I've dedicated myself to learning the timeless wisdom of spirituality and sharing it in ways that resonate with the modern soul. My journey has been a unique blend of the material and the mystical — a dance between the grounded world of tech and the infinite realm of spirit.

The Soulful Balance is more than a book; it is a piece of my heart. Within these pages, I've shared the lessons, reflections, and practices that have helped me align my outer world with my inner truth. My hope is that this book serves as a mirror for you — to awaken your light, embrace your authenticity, and live a life that flows with both purpose and peace.

This is my offering to the world. May it find its way to the ones who need it most.

With all my heart,

– Aashima

(God's Child)